STORY OF THE SOUL

STORY OF THE SOUL

Akhtar Naveed Syed

PARTRIDGE
A Penguin Random House Company

To order additional copies of this book, contact
Toll Free 800 101 2657 (Singapore)
Toll Free 1 800 81 7340 (Malaysia)
orders.singapore@partridgepublishing.com

www.partridgepublishing.com/singapore

CONTENTS

DEDICATION:

To my father, Syed Jalaluddin, and my mother, Anjum Jalal who have nurtured me and helped me believe in myself.

ACKNOWLEDGEMENTS:

My elder brother, Farhat Nasir Syed, helped me realize when to actually share my deepest feelings with the world.

My wife, Aniqa Bano, who has constantly shown me the path to be myself in the real world.

My niece, Sarah Syed, who gave me the confidence to go through the publication of this work.

1. AN ODE TO MY SOULMATE

Your head is blank

You don't have any feelings

All feelings are from heaven

But heaven is lost lost in the deep ocean

The oceans are beneath the seas yet the seas
themselves are beneath the oceans

The sea and the ocean are entangled to form a web

The spider forming the web is in my heart

My heart is soulless, my soul is mindless yet
who brought me to this is unknown

What is known is that I sold my heart to the seas

The mermaids make me insane yet my insanity is my ecstasy

What am I to do — my heart is burning, my
soul is bursting, my brain is melting

My demons drown me but my soul fights on in futility till the dawn

What is the dawn?

It is the resurrection of my soul

2. FACES ARE ENTRAPMENTS

Entrapments are the heart's snares

Endless strands of rays of hope

Strains of which enrich the soul

Power of these magnets is endless

Intense resonance pulls souls together

A stare is like a peak

A peak that is akin to a horizon

The view's alchemy steals hearts

The alchemy is the varied expressions

Faces are these soul-to-soul cupids

3. PIGEONS

Heaven's animals whose fate is unknown

Fate is a destiny whose cause is an enigma

The mystery of this phenomenon is known to all

However, the animals are too innocent to know

The birds' naivety predestines them to fail

This failure is a sorry tale

A tale whose tail is all curled up

The entanglements leave the birds to have nightmares

The dreams scare them to death

4. SCARECROWS

Humans made of straw

Shapes made of sunrays

Visions, which scare birds

Birds, which love to prey

Yet the predator becomes the prey

The predator is the flimsiest beast

The beasts are horrified by the sight

The sight is a dark shadow emanating rays of black magic

The magic's magician tricks the birds through a masked covering

The real prey dances with joy

The tricked and disillusioned beings hope death is near

Yet there's no death

All is well

It's just a matter of perception

The predators are blind

The fate of the blind is always being totally utterly deceived

5. THE SEAFARING PORPOISE

A messenger of hope, pleasure, fun, frolic and a merfolk

A being termed as saviour of the oceans

Oceans being his home

His companion being the mermaid queen

A queen who is his mistress, soul mate

The porpoise lives somewhere nowhere everywhere
except where his life's essence lives

Endlessly he looks for the one and only sweetheart
who resides in his heart soul and mind

The queen drifts in all times yet her mate is nowhere
but her soul knows he is very near

The porpoise lives in the Azores

The queen lives in the Indian Ocean

Their cupid resides in the Gulf of Oman

Their altar is at the cheetah's house

The cheetah awaits them with no worry for he is a fortune teller

6. THE KAZAKH FAIRY

A fairy whose beauty is mesmerising
She waits for her lover
The lover lives near Xiangi
The era is 1180A.D.
The two have never seen heard each other
They meet one another in their dreams
Their meeting place is Al Farabi's school of philosophy
The dreams are real
They hold arms kiss touch and feel each other
In real life they're melancholically drifting nowhere
One is a fortune teller on the road to Taklamakan Desert
The other lives near the fairies' lake
The lover is a dimension drifter
Al Farabi is their teacher, cupid and best friend
The fairy and the lover lie forever in bliss
Yet they dream in today's world

7. A WHALE'S EYE VIEW

The sea is as blue as the azure sky

The sky the sea floor

The rocks are the air

The air is in the water

The water is my home

My home is 10 nautical miles from The Cook Islands

The isles' are pristine

The untouched landmass welcomes all on its shore

The shore calls all beings to dance

The voodoo dancers set the rhythm

The ocean's rhythm is total brotherhood

My heart goes out to the soul sisters

The sisters are Anna, Maria, Firdosa

The seagull tells them where to find their lovers

Their lovers are Duncan, Marriot, Peter

They live 50 leagues under the sky

Near the Mariana Trench

8. THE FIRE BREATHING DRAGON

Fire is life

Life is hot cold molten frozen

The dragon is a sweet angel

The angel is a sweet radiant glowing source of light

The light takes my breath away

My breath smells of the succulent pieces of grass

Our charming dragon turned the tables

The fellow met his mate in the seas

The seas are their home

Their home is my home

But their home is miles away

Forever Mr & Mrs Dragon live peacefully

Their peace is never disturbed

Whoever tries melts

Hurrah for the great dragon

9. THE SEA SNAKE COUPLE AT PONAPE

The land of beautiful squids, octopus and ray fishes

Beings, which are harmless

The nearby sea snakes scare them

Yet Rosie and Ramdas have no idea why

The two never leave each other

They are soul mates forever

Have said that they have lost each other

Their mothers have been scared senseless

However, they reappear as if they were there forever

Their fathers knew all that

Thus they played with two jellyfishes

Rosie and Ramdas have no brothers no sisters yet they have five friends

Morn, Torn, Worn, Sorn, Dron are the five lucky seahorses

The sea snakes and the sea snakes love each other

The planktons are jealous, but who cares

10. THE SERENE BEACHES OF SEYCHELLES

As I saw the beach I was mesmerised

The view left me stunned

The schools of fish brought me to ecstasy

My ecstasy is soul deep

The jellyfish played voodoo music

Music, which was like heaven's harp

The harp was played by the breathtaking fairy

The fairy's eyes were scorching red

It blinded the blinded souls but brought sheer
joy to the souls without holes

The fairy hugged me forever

I will love her forever

I will miss her forever

I will yearn for her forever

I hope she will reciprocate

My wish is to go to the altar with her

Hope that we will be soul mates, playmates forever

11. THE ZAMBIAN TORTOISE

Is this a sea being from heaven?

No it may be a bird from paradise

The cat sniffed it

The 'pussy cat' hooted at it

The nightly stars stared at it

The papa bear knew what it was

The mama bear did too

And so did the big bear

Yet the baby bear couldn't believe what he was seeing

To him it was a Lilliputian gargoyle

A gargoyle that brought smiles to everyone's faces

All the faces lit up

All the lit up faces brimmed with joy

Their joy was destroyed when the angelic being disappeared

While disappearing it made no noise

Yet the 'pussy cat'

The cat was told but it too small to understand

12. THE MINSTREL OF SPAIN

My best friend since our times immemorial

He showed me Spain

It rendered no pain

Yet I felt saddened to the core

This mate of mine will and is with me forever

He is the best pest yet I am his pest

His being there is a surety

My being there is a rarity

However, my rarity is as good as his surety

What is good for him is good for me too

He has always shown me the way

His is the right way

For he follows the right path

As he is the minstrel of Madrid

His strange musings are my whisperings

All this is understood by no one

And I hope no one ever will

Yet our inheritors are staking their claim on the treasure chest

13. A PARAKEET'S MESSAGE

This is my best friend
Yet I could not save him from death
The cat ate him while I fought with the cat
But in my dreams he called
I was astonished for he did not admonish me
He just wanted me to meet his pal
I was afraid that his pal was a predator too
I tried unashamedly to stay away from his friend
However, in the end I had to meet him
He turned out to be an old friend of mine
Yet I did not recognise him
Only the parakeet told me he was my friend
When I went into a coma the clarity hit
Its glare sent me into a frenzy
In my mind I met this friend of mine
Who like me was in a coma too
Yet it was a meeting of minds
Now I don't want anything to change till eternity ends

14. TYPES OF GOATS

What are goats?
They are nothing but oats
What kinds of oats are they?
Both the worst and the best
They eat grass and fish in the same gulp
The fish eaters are the sea-goats
They work for the mermaids
The mermaids are their mistresses
These mermaids live in solitude
Hoping for the goats to bring a mate
But these goats are worthless
All they do is munch planktons
Even the planktons cry at the goat's misdemeanour
Yet the goats remain unashamed
However, the mermaids love these goats
For they provide them company
Which they yearn forever till time seizes
Yet if time seizes how will the goats breathe again

15. MESSENGERS OF FATES

Fates are soul's prisons

Prisons, which mar people's destinies

Destinies, which are lost forever

Even forever is a short time

For the forever is shortened by fates' messengers

These messengers live in heaven

Heaven is from where they observe all

As they are worthy angels

These angels help the soulless and the gutless

Those are those who have lost their souls forever

Till they are met by these angels

Angels, which help every soul except the dark ones

The dark souls destroy these angels

Their deeds are very good

The soulless souls thank them forever

16. FATELESS GUPPIES

Birds with no minds

But not mindless minds

The depth of their thoughts is intense

The intensity scares all the birds

Yet, being a humming bird, I feel no fear

The eagles and the vultures shy away from them

Their shyness is the cause

Their hearts have no fear

These guppies are not real birds

They are the sea's birds

They swim with octopus and sea anemones

No bird ever sees them

Except the kingfisher and the seagulls

These two nourish on the poor guppies

Yet if they were birds they would have been devoured by eagles and foxes

Being fishes is a small price to pay

As being in sea creature's intestines they still smell the briny air

17. TRAGEDIES ARE CUNNING

What is cunning?

Life is that

How can tragedies hurt one's heart?

By simple experiences

The cunning life cares for no one

Not a soul

All are left helpless

These helpless souls pray for a better life

Yet life is ever torturous

The torture tears minds

Such minds succumb to pressures

Pressures which are strange and mind boggling

Their strangeness causes the tenseness

No one is able to cope with them

All feel vanquished

Such is the defeat of the cunning tragedies

In this victory is the defeat of itself

All this exists only in my mind

18. A BEAR'S CRY

A soul deep cry of the wild
Not from the wild west but the east
It is an eastern howl
The sound, which sends chills down spines
But in the east it's the sound you dream to hear
This is so in the east as well as the north
The people in shark skins respect
The igloo dwellers think of them as teachers
One may ask who are they
They are whiter than snow
Are pinker than flamingos
Swim faster than sea dwellers
Come to think of it they are in the west too
They are the kings of the Arctic
Their presence brings an angel on the tundra land
The Eskimo keeps him as a pet
They posses a shrill cry for which his mate lusts after

19. THE EVIL WITHIN MANKIND

Mankind is truly sickening

I wish I was a spiritual being

A being, which stays in hearts, souls and all empty spaces

This evil burns my core

A core, which is so scarred that you cannot see the real face

The evil succumbs all people to become evil

This causes people to become nasty

All nastiness is unhamanly

Yet all mankind is nasty at times

What can be done?

Nothing it seems

Except waiting, hoping, praying that this evil disappears

However, this is no chance of that happening

As this evil is truly satanic

This virtue spoils mankind

One hopes it will disappear one day

20. A HEARTLESS SWORD

A swordfish's sword
Not heartless at all
Yet all fishermen think it as heartless
The sword is not a weapon
It is nothing but an instrument
It helps the maligned fish to hunt
The cries are heard by all
All fishes stay away from the swordfish
Though this fish loves all sea animals
It's a kind fish
It never pokes anyone with its probing sword
Yet no one likes it
Why would they like this sword?
Because of its innovativeness
No that too is a figment of imagination
All is all this sword is truly heartless
As it loves killing beings

21. A MINDBLOWING ROMANCE

The lovers are two whales
One lives in the Pacific
The other in the Arctic
Both know each other by letters exchanged
The letters are delivered by sonar mail
Their cupid is a flock of seagulls
The whole group transfers millions of mails daily
Both the whales are love struck
One of them decides to swim over
The passage takes her a week
Yet on reaching she finds he has left to find her
The sonar got jumbled
The whale swims back
On half way back the whales meet each other
Now they can't decide where to live
So they decide to meet a sage
The sage is bewildered too
He tells them it would be better leave one another

22. THE DANCING WITCHES

A tea meeting of out of this world
The tea served by two witches
One was a mermaid, the other a fairy
Both bewitched my core
Both talked to me telepathically
Each was conveying to me a message
My conscious became my unconscious
My dreams became my realities
All three of us were on such a carpet
A truly wondrous carpet
The wonder was how easily we were meeting mentally
The witches have friends
They are fairies
They, too, bewitched me
The fairies are my godmothers
So is the elder witch
The mermaid is my dream
But now my dreams are my dreams

23. THE BEAUTIES OF THE URALS

People ask me where are the Urals

Who knows I say

They look up the map of the Americas and can't find them there

I have a gig

For I went to the place 5,000 years ago

It was a campsite

The camp was of a circus

The circus had a theatre

The theatre had actresses, actors

The actresses were all beauties

I was the muse of these beauties

I helped them fall in love

Bringing sweet desires in their minds

Teasing their souls

Making them realise their men's desires

They could never thank me

For I died a moth's death

24. THE RUSSIAN SEDUCTRESS

She was of my friend's
My friend was her lover
Their love was great
She was this seductress
She had to tease and please him
Yet he never moved
He never fell in love
She tried, tried all in vain
He was my friend
He fell betrayed
For he thought she was my lover
He thought I fooled him
She too fell betrayed
They started to cast an evil spell
Yet they fell in love with each other
Now I became an evil cupid
However, I was his best man and her maid of honour
For all of us are earthworms

25. THE KING OF CUPIDS

Who are the cupids of this world?

Are they men, hen or women?

Do they live in pens or dens?

No to all

They live in nests

Do their work in the air

They are the lovely seagulls

In the water and the air they share their work

The land cupids are the owls

The water cupids are the sea anemones

Together they are magnificent cupids

However the king is the seagull

They plan it all

Hire the muses

Tame the beauties

Civilise the males

They have horns and spikes

Their lovers need muses too

26. THE SNOW LEOPARD OF KARACHI

Karachi is my hometown
So is it of my playmate
My playmate is a pigmy snow leopard
She lived with me for 50 years
I am a small ginger cat
The years are cat years
Both of us are still friends
She has gone on to heaven
But the fairies tell me of her
She was such a mean, lean, killing machine
She ate rats and I ate mice
She loved hunting hens and I parrots
Her friend was a black panther
Both of them played hide and seek
I was afraid of the panther
She was the panther's friend forever
Her master was a prince
A shrewd prince who loved her deeply

27. THE QUEEN OF BELLY DANCERS

She is a beauty from Corsica
Her dance is so exquisite
Her moves are mesmerising
All dancers try to ape her
Her complex renderings bewitch all
She is from a village
She loved moving her feet since age 1
Her father sent her to a dance coach on Barbary Island
The teacher was a good dancer
This queen lives 3,000 years from now
Her island is better than most places
Her students roam the world
Her fellow dancers, too, love her dance
She has hundreds of suitors
None please her
She desperately needs a muse and cupid
She now has found them
Yet she is yet to find her lover

28. THE EAST EUROPEAN ANGELS

These are five angels

They belong to the house of serpents

All five of them are exquisite pieces of beauty

Scores of men fancy them

Four are blondes, one is a black top

They'd love to have men too

As till now they have not gone to the altar

They are dancers in Taklamakan desert's oasis town

They travelled from Blaj in Romania

The Mongol horsemen and Chinese in caravans loved their dance

Of these angels one is my true love

I love her deeply

She knows this

But we still live apart

Our love is known to all five

Their teacher is between me and her

29. THE WARRIOR CHARIOT

This is Harriet's chariot
But who is Harriet?
She is an elf's maid
They live deep in the forest
The forest is enchanted
Gnomes also live there
Harriet is one of them
She helps soldiers of all sides
She rides on her chariot
Her horses are real stallions
She is the best nurse
She is perfect at her work
All sides laud her
Her chariot is irreparable now
She is inconsolable
She fell down broke her ribs
Her whole tale is so sorrowful
As she is at her death bed

30. THE DREAM MACHINE

A machine, which knows no bounds

Which passes through time

Passes through realms

All of which are real yet imaginary

The machine is everywhere

One uses it at sleep

When one awakens it shuts off

That's what life is all about

This machine nourishes

It replenishes souls

What if it always stayed on?

The dreams would be endless

So endless that there will be no realty

All reality would disappear

We would need no food and drinks

Yet some live their dreams

What if they could live their realities?

All will be different yet nothing will be different

31. THE SORCERER'S REVENGE

Who takes revenge?

Only a beast

What constitutes a beast?

Nothing but a body full of hate and conceit

What good is such a body?

Totally nothing

Yet, the sorcerer is right to take revenge

He is a humble sorcerer

His magic is a boon for all

I am under his spell

I am a tricked sea anemone

To get cured I am under his spell

He is not a monster as most think

He pleases me a lot

He used his powers on a fellow sea anemone

We are no more friends

She tried to kill me by a wizard's magic

I am thankful to the mighty sorcerer

32. THE HONEST LIAR

A liar who shares his soul

A soul, which meddles with everyone's lives

All are uneasy by his thoughts

The thoughts are unnerving and beguiling

However, he is a saint

He does all this in ignorance and innocence

Yet all blame him for this treachery

He is helpless

Yet he continues with his unadmirable ways

A seagull tries to tame him

She lures him to her nest

A nest full of eggs for him to care

However, he continues his ways

Showing her no respect

The liar is vanquished by a witch

He now turns into a sweet angel

33. THE PERSIAN PRINCESS

A princess with wings

Wings as beautiful as a peacock's

Her hair are golden

Her skin is dead white

She seduces no one

She gets seduced by no one

Her dreams tell her who her lover is

The lover too dreams of her

They live thousands of miles away

And they live in 5,000BC and 5,000AD

So how can they meet?

Except in their dreams

A doctor shows her the way

But the cure is useless

There is no cure

Only that the princess becomes a fairy

34. A TYRANT'S MURDER

Who murders who

A tyrant another tyrant

What's the use?

None

Really

Yes

No not at all

They both think they are right

Yet both are wrong

Both are sinful

Should go to hell

Though even hell will vomit them

They killed their souls

Now they are just agents of dark forces

They both plead innocence

But both will be punished equally

35. THE MUSLIN CLOTH

A cloth that holds life

As life ebbs away

My life is going away

I have no one to save me

Yet this tells me to hold on

That I do with utmost ease

The cloth is a family heirloom

It has saved endless souls

All souls are now in ecstasy

The cloth always hangs by the balcony

The balcony of the family's tomb

No one is afraid of it

Except Satan

He wants to have people murder themselves

But the heavenly cloth saves them

36. A DOLPHIN'S CRY FOR HELP

Help is in the saviour's hands

Hands, which are nine feet wide

The width engulfs all sorrows

The dolphin is helpless

Waiting for the whale of his dreams

His dreams are never fulfilled

Yet his dream whale swims in wait

His cry is an SOS

The call is that he seeks his whale

The whale is sure

What if she proposes?

Will the shy dolphin refuse?

She can't be sure

So she turns to a cupid

The cupid is a bird-cat of the sea

That is a sea-lioness

37. THE HELPLESS PRISONER

A prisoner who has lost his head

The headless person waits for his soul to depart

Yet that's taking time

Maybe the soul thinks the head will be reattached

A heavenly fairy comes to rescue the soul

The soul cries its heart out

The fairy and her pals dance around the head

Somehow the head is not detached

It was just a cut in the thread

The fairies are pleased to tell this to the soul

The prisoner wakes up but he has now lost his soul

It seems the soul has gone on a trip

A trip that may cost the prisoner's life

A life that may soon end

Yet the soul comes back within seconds

The prisoner's mind is thankful to the soul

38. THE MICROSCOPIC PLANETS

Planets in the head

The atoms of the soul

The electrons of the mind

The photons of the brain

They all are matter

They all rotate

All transform into energy

Energy that connects

The connection transfers souls

To the next stop

The brain to work

The mind to think

But do they exist

Sure they do

Otherwise what would be the point of living

These planets are real heavenly bodies

39. THE STARS THAT EVOKE DREAMS

Dreams that scare people

Tear their hearts into two

People who think too much

Thinking that breaks the dreams

Stars that bind the soul with the mind

The beauty of the stars befuddle all

Send people into a trance

Their naivety appeals to people

But that's the core of their beauty

Their thoughts please many

Most want to think like

But can't, as their hearts are blackened

Yet they cry for the star' attention

40. THE VOICE WITHIN

A soul deep voice

The voice of my heart

A heart, which has been crushed

The source of this torture is no one but another voice

That is my mind's voice

This voice suspends my soul

My soul yearns for my heart's voice

A voice to which all listen

My soul yearns for my heart's voice

A voice, which alarms me and even others

Both voices are my own

However, my self loves the mind's voice

For it's the sensible one

My soul is an irrational being

Thus it loves my heart's voice

A being, which is totally fanciful

41. THE MYSTERY OF THE SAINTS

These are the saints of paradise

They are angels of that habitat

They guide the mortal souls

They follow the commandments unquestionably

Their job is to guard paradise

The paradise is my ecstasy

This ecstasy can always be harmed by dark deeds and beings

These saints are my pals

They are in reality my thoughts

The rationale behind my decisions

Without them I would be nowhere

No, nowhere too would be somewhere

I would be in a bottomless pit

A pit inhabited by satanic beings

The mystery is only mine to know

42. MESSENGER OF DEATH

Death will come

Its messenger will bring it

This messenger is nothing but a feeling

A feeling from the heavens

A heart-felt notion

That makes one believe his fate

I already feel it

The feeling I feel is out of this world

It's a notion

Some fairies are calling

I once gave them my soul

They want me back

Yet I am stuck here

Here is my life

There is my death

43. THE HEARTLESS FOX

Not a sly fox

But a deadly fox

A fox who lives in the alleys of hell

A hellish being who has the vampire's habit

Even the vampire will be frightened by him

His heartlessness is famed

However the fame is of being murderous

Endless souls have been turned to dust by him

His end will come

His progeny will destroy him

They feel the hurt of the others

The fox knows this all

Yet he continues his merry ways

His ways are as satanic as Satan's

His fate is being tortured for him

Life is not enough, an eternity is!

44. CHAINS OF EMOTIONS

My emotions hurt me

The hurt is felt to my core

My core burns

The burning scars my soul

My scarred soul cries for help

Help comes from a Mauritanian beauty

Her eyes swell my heart

Her gaze un-scar my soul

My core finds a reason to live

Then she disappears

Yet she leaves behind in me a feeling to live on

However, I see she is there peeking from behind the cliff

Her presence is a gift for me

Her memories drive me on

Its nothing but a turn of emotions

45. A CRY FOR HELP BY THE WOMEN IN THE DUNGEON

Who are these women?

They are prisoners of their fate

They live in their heart's dungeons

Their dungeons are their prisons

Prisons, which force them to have no feelings

In their unconscious they cry for help

No one listens to these cries except the fairies

The fairies prey for these women

The women are my classmates

My stares imprisoned them

They lost feeling when I tricked them and conned them

The fairies know this

So they had me trapped by the queen

The queen is an evil mermaid

But one that is suitable for the heartless merfolk

46. A TIGER'S TAIL

A ten feet long tail

A tiger with a spider monkey's face

A spider monkey with a cheetah's fur

A tail with a tale of his own

No this is not a chimera

It is an Indian cheetah

Caught by the tail

By an uncle of mine

Who only saw the cat's tail

Maybe the tail was a piece of cloth

For I never saw it

Anyway, he kept it in his cupboard

So it has to be a cloth piece

No but he swore it was a tiger's tail

Sorry, I forget if it's a tiger or a cheetah

Anyway it will remain a mysterious tale

47. THE SAVIOUR OF THE DEATHS

Who is this saviour?

He is the dolphin of the poles

He helps men, porpoise and all other sea creatures

A small dolphin with a big heart

A heart that saves souls from murders

The murderers are the ships

Ships of oils and pesticides

The deaths are of planktons, fishes and sharks

The dolphin needs the help of the seafaring porpoise

They together help these souls

However, both of them look for their mermaids

Their mermaids, too, are helper creatures

All such beings are the saviours

The beneficiaries pray for them

They only want to save more lives

48. COMRADES IN ARMS

Three dear friends holding hands in hand
All swam and played by the sea
The sea shells pricked
They did not mind that
For them it was acupuncture
As they frolicked the dolphins swam by
They were fascinated
They were mystified
Seeing this the dolphins jumped with joy
They look like flying fish
The comrades were left stunned
Their astonishment made the sea laugh
The laughter of the waves made the buddies shudder
In their frightened state they returned to their golden chariots

49. THE PURPLE PRIEST

A Levi priest

A true saint

Who lives in Ethiopia

But is not his homeland

His homeland is between Baghdad and Cairo

The Coptics despise his tribe

Yet they prosper

In their success they belittle all

This treachery angers all

However, in the parallel universe where I live
in they are not Levis but just crows

This universe is ours

The crows, too, are despised

In cities they abound

Where they belittle the other birds

Birds with mindblowing whistles

50. THE SEDUCTRESS AND HER SLAVE

The slave is an ape

The mistress is his slave

Her slavery knows no mounds

The bounds limits' are so wide

The width lets them discover each other

The seductress is the mistress

The slave brings offerings to this goddess of his

The goddess continues to tease him

He loves to be teased

For he is so enraptured by her spell

No she is not a witch

Yet her magic brings peace to his heart

She is a chimp who has ensnared this ape

This ape loves his fate

51. THE SERENE HORDE

A horde so beautiful

Yet so miserable

All the members are depressed

This depression is felt by all

Yet their keeper sees that they stay like this

This misery is not a misery

It is a misery with a twist

A twist, which enchants the hordes

They feed on particles in the sand

With a vengeance seen in no beast

All beasts are envious of them

But their jealousy does not bother these sweet gargoyles

These angelic beings are beautiful to watch

52. THE SPRINGS OF NEVADA

Is it Nevada or Adaven?

Adaven sounds funky

This land is near the Mariana Trench

From where the Barbarry pirates reach the oldest world

This is the one Jules Verne discovered

All laughed at this suggestion

Yet this Duke Barbosa is the commander of that land

Where sea monsters abound

Dinosaurs talk to manatees

Ostriches make love to dodos

Here all women have light coloured eyes

For they are witches

Witches who have stolen Barbosa's heart

Who is so so in love

The springs here are of pure white milk

53. THE SUPERSONIC ANGELS

A beacon in the sky

The sky reaching to the seventh heaven

It lighted when I reached the gate of hell

Where the enchantress' island lies

The island is where I was born

My birth was scary as hell was near

But our tribe of seducers is used to that

Through these angels we connect with others of our tribe

They all live in other galaxies

We all are the keepers of the underworld

Which is guarded by the Amazonias of Deccan

They are fairies

Back on earth to defend the universe

Or is it a multiverse?

54. THE WATERY GRAVE

Where is this?

Is it the Noah's floods deads' remains

No, it's the remnants of a storm

A storm that hit paradise

A paradise in the sky

Which leads to Atlantis

The tombs are of the angels, fairies and troll who guard this path

Who initiated this storm?

A demon who is in league with satan

Now this land has been replenished

Can one control these forces of darkness?

By seeking the charmed ones in Mu

Where is Mu?

Somewhere in the Pacific Ocean

55. A SIREN'S PRISONER

Prisoner of her soul

Soul of a siren

Siren so bewitching

Her sight entrances all

All who despise her

All who love her

She is a witch

A witch of the seas

A sea where the prisoner lives

Her prisoner is a merman

A being who loves her

Yet she tortures him

A practice he loves

His heart is hers

She gives him her virginity

A state so divine

A divinity he steals

Now he wishes to worship her

She teases him endlessly

He loves the feeling

56. MERMAIDS OF MY DREAMS

Dreams made in heaven

Heaven made of water

Water in the sky

Sky on the ground

Ground so high above

A place so serene

A serenity of sirens

Sirens that I love

Love of the mermaids

Mermaids who possess me

An ownership I cherish

A pleasure so resounding

Yet I never dream

The dreams are of a siren

A siren of paradise

The paradise where I live

Life full of pleasure

Pleasure the mermaids seek

The mermaids are my soul mates

Mates who are in my dreams

57. LOVERS OF MY DREAMS

Lovers who love to tease

A teasing that I love

Yet I never find love

Love that is in my dreams

Dreams that I see

The vision is in my dreams

Yet I am awake

An awakening so comatose

A slumber, which I love

A love full of lovers

Lovers who are sirens

Sirens who are goddesses

I am their slave

A slave for eternity

A time in my dreams

Dreams that never end

An ending that never comes

Yet I wait

A waiting so short

Pleasured by the lovers

58. MERMAIDS OF INDUS

A river so pure

A purity so divine

Divinity that houses goddesses

Goddesses that are virgins

Virginity so pristine

A wildness so seductive

Seduction of the sirens

Sirens worshipped by the dolphins

Dolphins so blind

Men who love the sirens

Sirens tease them

Sirens are hated

Men lose their souls

Souls so dark

Darkness hated by the sirens

Sirens of my existence

They are my mates

Mates whom I worship

For I am a dolphin

A being so in awe of the sirens

59. MERMAIDS OF CASPIAN

A sea of my vision

Vision that I see

A sight in my hallucination

My brain in a trance

An affect of the sirens

Sirens of the sea

Sea so salty

The sirens love the salt

Salt that they relish in

Men are so afraid of them

They lose their souls to them

Souls so devious

The sirens so pure

A purity felt by the salmons

Salmons who are their slaves

Slaves who worship them

They ensnare the men

Men who are the devil's incarnate

An existence so hideous

A fact hated by the mermaids

60. MERMAIDS OF MY LIFE

Life as a slave
Slave of serenes
Serenes so seductive
A seduction so pleasing
A pleasure I seek
Serenes that ensnare me
An entrapment so divine
A feeling so mesmerising
An existence so loving
A love of the serenes
Who are my mates
Mates so sweet
Who are my goddesses
Goddesses whom I worship
They are my life's purpose
Purpose so nice
An existence so soothing
A feeling the sirens love
Love shared by me
For I am so in a trance by their ways

61. MY ENCHANTING DREAMS

Dreams sent by fairies

Fairies of Thiarca

Thiarca of Homer

Homer in my dream

Dreams so so enchanting

A spell so entrancing

Fairies whom I seek

I am besotted by one of them

The fairies visit me

My dreams are so vivid

A clarity that brings ecstasy

A feeling so refreshing

An awakening so intense

An intensity so heart felt

The fairy is a mermaid

A siren so serene

Her serenity allures me

A seduction in dreams

Dreams I see endlessly

Yet she is never there

62. PARADISE OF MY DREAMS

Dreams sent by mermaids

Mermaids to whom I am enslaved

A slavery so worthwhile

I am so ecstatic

A feeling so cherishing

The joy I see in my dreams

Dreams made in paradise

Paradise full of mermaids

Mermaids whom I love

A love so intense

Whose strength is so endearing

My pleasures are endless

The paradise is my home

Home where I live

A life full of dreams

Dreams of my soul mates

Mates who are mermaids

Creatures so divine

I savour their matriarchy

Yet I yearn to reach this paradise

63. THE GODDESS SIREN

A siren from Siberia

Siberia in heaven

A being so beautiful

Beauty in the eyes

Eyes so green

A colour of the witch

Her eyes frighten all

Yet some are seduced by her

A feeling they love

Her shape is so divine

Her worshippers love to please her

A pleasure she loves

Her subjects love her appearance

An appearance from heaven

She being a goddess

A goddess of the world

World she created

A creation loved by all

She loves to tease all

All who love her ways

64. THE MERMAID'S LOVER

A lover who is a water being

A being so sweet

A sweetness so innocent

An innocence the mermaid loves

A love he loves

Their love blossoms

Fruits are shared

They reach ecstasy

Yet he despises her

For she loves others

Others whom she treasures

She loves to tease him

He hates her

Yet she pleases him

Her lovers are all mermaids

Mermaids so treacherous

He is scared of them

They too seduce him

He becomes their lover

His mate now imprisons his soul

65. THE WICKED MERMAIDS

Sirens of hell

Hell that is their prison

Prison of lava

Lava so hot

Hell they love

Love so soul deep

Souls so impure

Dirt so deep

Depth so scary

A sight hated by all

Their ways so devious

Yet they're so sweet

The beings of hell love them

They worship them

For they are their goddesses

Goddesses of fire

Fire of devil's existence

Existence so heart breaking

A sight so breathtaking

A feeling so unnerving

66. POSERS ARE HYPOCRITES

Hypocrites of thoughts

Thoughts of actions

Actions concealed

Concealed as in veiled

Veiled by slyness

Slyness that poses

Poses to be true

Truth that is false

False as a poser

Poser as a freethinker

Thinking not

Not as in human

Human that is closed

Closed as a path

Path that are his thoughts

67. FEAR OF FEAR

Fear of thoughts

Thoughts that unnerve

Unnerve my mind

Mind full of ideas

Ideas of passion

Passion for a cause

Cause for a struggle

Struggle of mankind

Mankind in need of my ideas

Ideas for sharing

Sharing to bring change

Change that many fear

Fear that must be erased

I *Miss* YOU

ABOKSAN

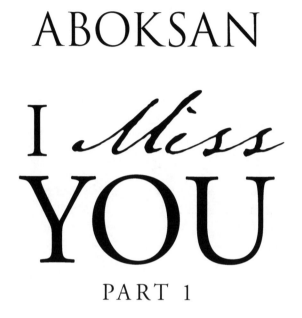

I *Miss* YOU

PART 1

(COLLECTIONS OF POEMS AND
SHORT STORIES FROM ABOKSAN)

PARTRIDGE
A Penguin Random House Company

To order additional copies of this book, contact
Toll Free 800 101 2657 (Singapore)
Toll Free 1 800 81 7340 (Malaysia)
orders.singapore@partridgepublishing.com

www.partridgepublishing.com/singapore

**This booklet
is dedicated**

To

....

....

....

**with a message of
I miss you alot**

From:

....

....

....

For My Loving Wife Emily Francis Asing and
Our loving sons, daughters and grandchildren

Also to Emmanuel, Rachel and Jonathan Jethro

WHO HAS BEEN THE SOURCE OF MY JOYS
AND REASON TO LIVE IN THE LORD!

Life is an experience . . .
Experience can be painful but
pains make man thinks;
Thought makes man wise and
Wisdom makes life endurable.

. . . Estonella W. J. M (1973)

Contents

1

The Way We Were

(Composed on: 15th June 1975.
Recomposed on: 21st Mac 1997)

Beautiful Sunday. That was my first **lonely day** ever since I had gone **across the universe** down to **San Francisco.** As I drew near the window, I heard a **voice in the wilderness** beyond the **country**-side.

"**Michael . . .**" It whispered from the **morning glow** . . . **release me** and **leave me alone** . . . alone . . ."

Then I came to realise that voice echoed from **you,** the only **woman in my life.** I could not help myself **crying in the rain.** I felt **so sad** that I raced out of my room into the vast **cotton field** without looking at **a whiter shade of pale.** The splashes of the **cool water** did not stop me from running. As I climbed up **around the bend** and missed my steps. I fell **like a rolling stone** down the hill on the **summertime blues.**

For a minute or two, everything was quiet except for the **chirpy chirpy cheep cheep** sound made by the **tiny sparrow**, a **yellow bird** that rested on a branch of **lemon tree** closed by.

Slowly I dragged myself among the **green leaves of summer** and lent my back on the **evergreen tree** beside the **moon river.** "**I can't help it**", I said to myself as I wiped my tears from my **ebony eyes.** It was all over for you had **gone,** leaving me alone in the **silent night.** And I sat there watching the **clouds** driven by **four strong winds** across **New York City.**

"*The* **shadow of your smile** cast upon the **middy sun** as the **song of joy** to me. Now that *I've* **lost you**, how come you say: **it doesn't matter to me**" I then cried in **sorrow** without any **suspicious minds.** "Oh, my **sweet little Jesus boy** . . . what a sorrowful memory of mine . . ."

It was like *a daydream*, yet it was true. *If* I had known it before, I could have joined *the boxers* in the *revolution* against the *evil ways*. And should I die, at least I had said *the soldier prayer*. I hate to leave you before but *mother* said we were *too young to be married* before *you're sixteen* at that time. That was why I went to *San Bernardino* for my further study. Now that my *elusive dream* was broken, I could feel my life like *one bad apple* that had been mixed *over and over* in the *circle game*. I did not have the *silver treads and golden needle* to sew my broken heart in the *unchained melody*. But I refused to be another *proud Mary* and ended as *Tom Dooley*. Because, all I had in my life is you, *Stoney* who was last seen in the *season of the sun*.

As I woke up with the *sunshine on my shoulder*, I knelt down and prayed: "Lord, *take good care of my baby,* please". So for the first time in my life, I walked in between *fire and wind* which was *blowing in the wind*. A Comanche from the *Indian reservation* charged on my way but I fought them all and won just like what you told me once, "Friend . . . *keeps yourself alive!*" I could not have a *free ride* on the *48* crash horse so I sent my *butterfly* with a *photograph* telling you I was on my way home to say *hello darling*. In the meantime, I would *walk a mile in my shoes* before I sailed down the *Mississippi* river for the next *five hundred miles.*

I had bought a *ticket to ride* on the flying machine under *Helen wheels* for home which was still *half a million miles from home* before I came to the *top of the world*. Without entering the *house of the rising sun*, I paid a visit on the *china grove* beside the *yellow river* where we had our *last song together*. I slept there as a *rainy day man*. Half slept in the *summer sand*; I was awakened by the sound of the *jingle bells*. I heard a voice crying, "*Here comes Santa Claus!*"

"Hello boy . . . *I've a plan for you!*". He said but I ignored it. "Come on, *Danny Boy*. Does anybody really know what time it is?"

I shook my head like a *blind owl*.

"Oh . . . , my boy, it's a *Blue Christmas!*" He then laughed and danced with the *Dancing Queen*.

However, this did not change my mind. Instead we were *hurting each other*. But then I felt a soft hand touched my weary shoulder from behind the ark tree. I turned and to my dear surprise it was *you,* my honey. "*Can this be real . . . ?*" I wondered in awe.

You then smiled and said, ". . . Welcome home!" For the first time you kissed me with tender kisses then the *last kiss* we had before.

We burst into laughter and together we repeated our *evergreen* promise. "*I won't last a day without you*! For the *end of the world* had gone forever".

"*Don't forget to remember* cos *I'll never fall in love again* but you", I whispered as *me and you and a dog named boo* raced across the *green green grass of home*".

*Those appear *in italic* are names of songs.

2

Place of Love

(Composed on: 18th August 1975)

Near a stream, up a cliff
Among the bamboo trees, there I lie
Never the road that bends on my left
Where I walk for a while
    Amongst the flowers, beside the deadly thorn
    So as my heart that feels tired and worn.

Beside the river, beneath the trees;
And watch the moon far away that shines
As I whisper her name in the evening breeze
And hope that it reaches the other lines
    And yet her name seem new and fresh,
    Since those happy days that never again to rest

Along the margin of the riverside
With pasture that stretches for a mile or least;
Especially the blue and wild flowers on its side
Which remains me of her all the best
    But the robin and cicada never again to chirp
    For this place, never again she makes another trip

As the sun set and the dew is heavy
That drops on my eyes and washes away my tear
Suddenly I feel happy and never again seem weary
Because you told me before never to shed tear
    For you'll go and you'll be back again
    And starts the joy that you and I have shared

3

Winnie, The Boss of May

(Composed on: 1st September 1975)

As the dawn rolls by, emerge a new day,
With winds blowing in the day of May;
"Cos no one understands except you and me
What a boring month for Winnie and me
Bit I don't care how it all goes,
Knowing that you'll never be a ghost,
Even though you appear to be the boss,
Sending me away like a ship in the sea that lost.
Yesterday, today and tomorrow is another say,
But whenever I saw you, with all my might and way
Giving away I hate to say,
Like a friend used to do every January,
Lastly but not the least of me,
I'ould like to say something to Winnie;
Though I was the winner and yet I said it wasn't me,
"Cos' we'll meet her again someday behind the house of a limey.

4

An Advice
(Dedicated to the "Unhappy")

(Composed on: 12th September 1975)

I sighed and yet I did not
Shed a tear to you, my friend,
How can I said: "I dare not",
For my heart bleeds to pitiness,
You said, you are in miseries,
With worries, guilty of stupidity,

But you have forgotten the Bible my dear friend,
You are stupid and yet not so foolish;
You are worried and yet not so harass;
You are guilty but not yet proved;

For always remember that you still have hope,
To forget the past and start a fresh,
With Faith, Hope and Love,
But the greatest of all is Love.

5

Gone

(Composed on: 17th September 1975)

Gone . . . .
There go all my sweet dreams,
A dream to share my world with you,
But now, I can't call it my dream anymore,
"Cos you have walked away from me . . . . ,
Without word and no reason,
Though I keep on asking my self;
Why should you break my last hope?
Could you tell me the reason, why?

Gone . . .
You never know how much I hate that word,
Not even for the third and the last time.
But can't help it since that's my fate . . .
Probably my last fate and never again to recover . . . .

6

New Year Hope

(Composed on: 10th October 1975)

What a gracious time of the year to say;
Hello friend! What a sweet year for us to foresee,
With joys, new hope, love of friendship written for a tale;
But as for me, I have a promise ages ago to fulfil,

To recall the past is what I love much,
Suit enough for a little poet, who was born on March,
But on this day, to recall a friend is as good as it can be;
Cause the love of friendship stays like a mother and her baby,

Well friend, there goes the old, unforgettable year,
In which I promised you a hand to bear,
Maybe you said, "He breaks his promise on that day"
But as for me: A promise is a promise 'tho there's a delay,

Ahead are "Fire and Rain" though I can only guess and hope to win,
In spite of those: Let us pray that our friendship will be preserved
without end.

7

Power of A Girl

(Composed on: 3rd November 1975)

One morning I whispered, "Where is Irene?"
And they all murmured like toads in the rain
"You foolish guy, I told you to get lost!"
Said someone who sat beside my dearly host.
    My cheek turned red and felt my heart beat
    And swore in my heart that I'ould tear him to bits.

But before I could hit, someday gripped my feet
And said, "Please be patient or you'll lose your teeth"
On hearing the mock, they all laughed at me,
And discovered the coolness of water they threw at me . . .
    I couldn't help myself so I begged my humble host
    As you let me go home on a saddle without a horse.

As I walked alone the insults rang in my ears
And dedicated to stay there no matter how many years
How I swear to take a revenge on him;
But they all faded away when she said, "forgive him"
    You may wonder how I fought the evil and won
    'cos' I always believe the soft voice of my girlfriend . . . . Alone!!!!

8

Lonesome

(Composed on: 23rd February 1976)

Lonesome
That's what I feel wherever I think of you girl
I feel as if I'm a stranger from afar

Each morning my love glow brighter in my heart
Each day my heart always bleeds of you
Each night I always dream of you
But most of all I still feel lonesome

For you have gone and left me through the storm
You say you need me as your friend of street
Yet yesterday you said you have never known me
It breaks my heart before I ended up as a lovelorn.

9

The Blame

(Composed on: 1st March 1976)

Friend someone must take the blame
No matter whether you are a black or gentle lamb
Each day and night that elapse
With tender kisses from your sweet lips
Filling my heart in a dream of mine
A hidden treasure within my mind

Though you've never show me a sunrise
But sunset which fades in the west
Yet I thank you for hurting me more
As long as I love yesterday and tomorrow

The old years has gone, the new years comes
Still you have not given me a simple welcome
But whatever happens that isn't your fault
Never be in a billion years to come

    For the blame in my heart that itches
    Move my love in every minute and inches

One morning I whispered, "Where is Irene?"
And they all murmured like toads in the rain
"You foolish guy, I told you to get lost!"
Said someone who sat beside my dearly host.
    My cheek turned red and felt my heart beat
    And swore in my heart I could tear him to bits.

But before I could hit, someday gripped my feet
And said, "Please be patient or you'll lose your teeth"
On hearing the mock, they all laughed at me,
And discovered the coolness of water they threw at me . . .

10

A Broken Heart

(Composed on: 22nd Mac 1976)

Friend . . .
I don't understand why this heart of mine is
Keep on throbbing as the time passes by
Making the world whirl with emptiness
No rhythm, no peace within my mind
Honestly, I said as a genius . . .

That yesterday I was on top of my class
With pride and happiness camouflaged my sorrow
For I lost her but I still have you

For yesterday has gone and never again to show up
Though I begged you to think twice but you said
"That isn't important for me", and you walked away,
Making another, to make a thousand knot of my broken heart . . . .

11

I Wonder

(Composed on: 22nd April 1976)

I wonder why must there be a ceaseless storm
That makes my heart to cry for your love
Is it because the beginning of my doom
Which you've send flying with the dove?

I wonder if I make a mistake
To kiss your photograph before I sleep
Hoping that my hands you'll take
And tread the waves with a double leap
I wonder what you have got to say
When I say "I'm sorry forgive me'"
Will you tell your friend and see
"Poor guy, he must have a nightmare"

And lastly . . . I wonder
If you'll knock at my door again
Though you never think it yonder
But I love to recall it again and again

12

Hidden Love From Memory

(Composed on: 28nd April 1976)

Someone next door used to say: Hey!
Whenever I meet her in the morning
So graceful, pretty and yet so high
In moral: a gift from the Beginning
And she was my friend, Estonella
Who used to stay next to my villa

I don't really know how it all started
Is it because we hailed from the same school
Or is it the love which we once have started
But she denied it so as to let my heart cool

She would forget all about it in due time
But to a guy like me it fades no more
Because they're the gift of all time
Throughout my life and death to my fate
But I shall go on loving her cos' of my faith.

13

Wisdom

(Composed on: 29th April 1976)

No joy without peace in mind
Like gold hidden inside a mine;
Wihout light to guide the way;
Like a frog inside a metalware.

With the rain falling down heavily,
And fades its colour like a lily;
With no more hope to be bright and gay,
Thus end your life in a useless way

By and by you still have a nice day,
To say hello! And feel the happy day;
On which you turn to be a new leaf,
And do things that you hate to leave.

14

Votes of Thank

(Composed on: 30th April 1976)

No one can expect to meet a young guide
With a sweet smile that she can not hide
So gentle and petty that's all I can convey
Other that the girl from the Department of Lands and Survey
Without her, it would be another boring tour and day
But thanks God! I made it all right thru' out the day

Looking up the sky, you can tell that was a nice Friday
Especially with friends from Francis Convent, half the day
Who smiled and joked but I had forgotten to ask their names
I just couldn't do so 'cos they were anxious for my real name.
Anyway whoever you're: Thanks for everything plus care
Especially the one who approved my poems to be okay,

As the sun set for a short rest in the west
I clapped my hands in silence and for a rest
To my classmates, staffs, guide and loving friends
For they deserved to have a bright night without rain.

15

Just for A Smile

(Composed on: 1st May 1976)

There are times to say, Hello,
Yet not time to bid goodbye;
As if you humble yourself low,
That the time refuses to pass by;
And we walk along the golden coast
With a green carpet of grass on its side;
Without realising, how much it costs;
When someone take you from my side
And send me away like a gypsy love-lorn,
Crying and waiting in the rain all alone;

Never thought it would happen in dawn of May,
Because I always love you and come what may;
In case you changed your mind for a smile,
Before you send away from home, a hundred miles.

16

A Dedication

(To Estonella)

(Composed on: 24th August 1976)

Time has passed so quickly
That I don't have time to delay
To see you and greet you today
On your nineteenth birthday.

As a bud, as a flower that blooms in the morning
So as life that is full of sweet dreams and learning
To see you how you grow up to be a young lady
Although from far away where I always dare
With my hands clapped close to my dear heart
For you to be friendly and always work hard

No promise nothing whatsoever
Even hard feeling that never
Except for one thing that's dear
Remember me today in a year.

17

Gone With The Wind

(Composed on: 30th August 1976)

When I was young I had a dream
    Of someone I always will
But life was then like a rim
    That turn with the wheels
We grew up like the Children of God
    Who know what is love
But she changed her mind for she've got
    Antother friend she she always love
Half a decade has gone by but then
    I am a fool to wait for her
But I will not give up until Lent
    Cos that's the day I met her
And try not to make her love twin
    Eversince it has gone with wind.

18

Something to Ponder About . . . Love

(Composed on: 29th August 1976)

Love is patient and kind, love is not jealous or conceited or proud, love is not happy with evil but is happy with truth. Love means you never say you're sorry. Love is not ill-mannered or selfish or irritable. Love never gives up: its faith, hope and patient never fail.

Yet countless more has not been mentioned.

Take a good look around you: You will see lovers walking hand in hand. You will hear someone is whispering. I love you. You will not ask why must a dove flies and settle in pairs. Probably you will give a little smile when you see a sticker, poster or T-shirt with the word: Love beautifully printed with colours of rainbow or sunset on it.

All these are familiar to you because you hear them ringing and see them on papers everyday. And if you are lucky, you are probably one of those who composed them. But the questions are: How far is love means to us? Who are supposed to be in love, for what reason? Who give you love? When love means scarification, does it effect someone's life in misery? Lastly have you a love or more precisely: has the world a love?

You may think me as a crazy fellow in asking what a common and silly questions. But, have you think it deeply before you figure out—because I am thinking of a friend of mine who used to be a modern Romeo but now has turn to be another Casanova. To those who beat their heart and say: "I will stay where you left me . . ." To someone who whispers," Oh God, she can't do this to me . . ." To those who are ignorant of love and pitiless. To all damned killers and murderers. And lastly to those who love to see a bird with a wounded wing.

Among us, many are subjected to disappointment because of love. There are things like hatred, torture and crime all around us. Yet there are also thing like mercy and love which gives us hope to behold our future. And if you are looking for peace in mind, everlasting richness, unlimited happiness: Please do not look for materialism but true love. For God says," Faith, Hope and Love but the greatest of all is love!"

Well . . . How about you my friend?

19

Prayer In Memory

(Composed on: 6th November 1976)

Since the day you've gone across the sea
Far away from homeland, mummy and me
I've nothing to behold but our memories
The smile that you gave to a guy like me
Sometime I think I am just another crazy . . .
Gazing our last photo with my dreamy eyes
With my jilted heart far away from my soul
Yet as the new day emerge from the misty light
My heart begin to miss a few but two beats
Hoping and praying for you to be alright
For another day till you return home again.

20

. . . Just A Feeling . . . .

(Dedicated to all my friends wherever they may be)

(Composed on: 6th November 1976)

It reminds me of my feeling
Of missing another gentle lamb;
But it has to be 'thou I forbid,
Like a gentle bee that has to lead;

To me you are one of my best friends,
Although we seldom talk and joke
But enough to make me cry in the rain,
Especially when you refuse to sweep;

Anyway that is okay with me
So long as you keep on smiling
To all our friends and then me,
Lest I forget and list you missing;

May the happy day rise to meet you
And linger the memory we have gained;
Although I hate to say goodbye to you,
Hoping that one fine day we will meet again.

21

A Distant Call

(Composed on: 20th January 1977)

Alone, I sit by the steep riverside
In a kingdom where a prince resides
A poetic call comes from nowhere
Across the sea where my heart lay

    It is a mockery but gentle invitation
    That seeps through the Atlantic Ocean
    "You don't have to be sit and lie there
    Far away from her whom you really love
    So why don't you swear a solemn wish,
    To be hobo before you decide to drift west

Tear drips from my ebony eyes
Because I have never asked her: Why?
It comes again once in a little while
Make my prudent little heart going wild.

22

Dawn of My Magnanimous Life

(Composed on: 1st February 1977)

Sit Back, Speak Up and Look Honest
Yet nothing helps when life is a misery
As if the sunshine comes from the west
Making my life fickle and prudent mystery;

I can **sit back** and pretend to be sailor
Close my eyes and think of the blue door
In spite of what I am—a guy below,
The richness of this world which man adore,

I can't **speak up** all my untold grief
For every whisper is but a great load
Like a giant wave against the grey reef
Which I myself don't understand but Lord;

Do I **look honest** despite of all my guilt?
How I try to find a friend instead of you
Thanks, for now I know she isn't a light
That led to the altar but only you.

Sit back, speak up and look honest
What a whisper to put off my shame
But I leave it up to you, my dearest
In the meantime, life is still the same

23

Saturday Evening Tragedy

(Composed on: 26th February 1977)

It was Saturday evening. The silver-mingled sun lights were peeping among the dark green leaves of the tall palm trees. Several stray golden rays shone against the grey wall of the old church. Still some escape right through the transparent windows, opened doors and arches as it spread along the aisles. It was a notable scene.

The congregation who filled the hall took little notice of it. To them it was nugatory. They were more concerned with the happy and lively man-made atmosphere. For it was a blessed occasion especially for a man and a woman. What a consecrated mass! Looking at their faces, joys and happiness were written. Indeed, it was a worth-sharing evening both to the old and the young. Even to the little kids. Yes, to every soul who witnessed the gathering; all except one.

On the right corner of the last pew beside the aisle seated a young man. He was wearing a posh blue shirt and a black trouser with a polished dun boot. A batik neck-tie hugged on his colour earned him the respect as a natty youth. Silence fell on him as he listened to the buzzing whispers from the grateful guests. Some talked about handsome groom; others mentioned something nice of the cute bride. Still another matched them as a right partner. Nothing ill was spoken of them, instead all the heavenly blessings that ever bestowed on earth, they had them. It reminded him the early days of their courtship.

That was the time he came to know her. They were then schooling in an English school near the same church. He was seventeen and she was a year younger. It was truly a memorable evening; the school field was packed with students undergoing their hard training for their annual school day. Laughter rang and filled the scene. Several senior students were running and jolting in and along the tracks; whilst others preferred to fool around rather than be serious. Yells and gossips could be heard from the four sides of the field. Small children cried as they were bullied by the naughtier ones. Yet, that was only a part of the vivid school life.

Due to certain circumstances (or was it fate), the captain of his house was not there that evening so being the vice-captain, and he took his place. As usual, he guided his proud Blue House members on to a routine of familiar exercise and training before they were allowed to have their own choice of game. Everyone tried to make used of their own initiative for better performance. In fact, they had a bright chance to defence their championship title for another successive year.

With a little luck, he hoped to win half a dozen medals for his collection. He was energetic, good sport boy, courteous but quite lenient. Those characters of his had been known to all his schoolmates. This, a bunch of girls took advantage of his visible weaknesses. They asked for an hour break which then lasted that whole evening. Strangely, he neither regretted his leniency nor disliked those naughtier friends of his.

As he had to record the reasons, he approached them individually and politely. At last, he came to a pretty, shy-looking and modest girl; his charming Esther.

He still remembered how he bid her gently; "Hello girl! Aren't you feeling well? Would you care to join us for a short training?"

Esther gave a sweet smile as she said," I don't know . . . I just don't like to play . . ." It was a naive reason but it did not end there for another question was asked. So it dragged on. They sat together on the green grass under the shade of a palm tree from the fading light of the sunset.

How he wished the sun never set that day for it was the shortest evening of all. No wonder he neglected his task the first time in a year. Notwithstanding the long night, the Lord granted his prayer when he met her the next morning with a nosegay for her.

It was a nonplus to her dream. Since then, they were always seen together walking, joking and playing as a close pal. Too close for an ordinary teenager. They had a dream to build.

After the graduation day, they stopped seeing each other frequently. Esther found a job in the next town whilst he was still engaged with his studies in a high school. Nevertheless, they still met twice weekly. Late one evening, he met her on the same place outside the church for the last time.

"Esther, please don't be sad. I'll come back for you to have our dream fulfilled as soon as I get my Honours Degree. That's a promise, Honey!"

Esther could not utter a word. Her heart was, disconsolate as her tears dripped from her eyes. He reached for his handkerchief and wiped off her tears longed before he kissed her goodnight and goodbye. The following morning, he flew off to Sydney with a solemn whispered;" Esther, please wait for me; I'll come back to marry you someday!"

He did not realise that those last words came out of his dry lips. No one heard it. The sound of the organ filled the hall and the congregation stood up as the bridegroom walked gracefully along the golden-colour nave towards the candle lighted and inflorescent altar. He stretched his feet, in time to have a glance of the cute familiar face of the bride.

The bride was Esther in person. He felt the warm sweet flowed from his forehead. His feet grew weaker and weaker onto a state of collapse.

He fought and won with all his remaining might, at least for the time being. No one saw his strange behaviour except the bowing statue of Christ that hung on the cross behind him.

"Esther, do you take this man to be your husband?" With a clear and eager voice, she admitted willingly. "Yes, I do!" Those words seemed to echo in his head louder and louder. It was too much for him. It shattered his heart, hope and dream. Slowly, he realised that Esther was no longer his.

Without a word, he left the congregation and walked to the little hut behind the dark shadow of the church. It was there where they used to meet for the last seven years. He could hardly get behind it when he felt the dark mist on his eyes.

He clamped on the rotten wall as he fought for breath. He was suffering from paroxysm heartbreak both physically and spiritually. His feet were cold and numb.

At last, he raised his weary head towards the main church door; there walked Esther with her handsome husband to the waiting Mecedesbenz car. He tried to shout for help but in vain.

". . . Goodbye Esther, I'll see you in Heaven then . . . ." was his last word before he bowed his head to rest forever. No one wept for his. Not that cold Saturday evening.

24

Dawn of Life

(Composed on: 30th Mac 1977)

It was twilight. The blue sky was changing from a reddish grey to a dark blue. The moon had not yet risen behind the string of mountains far away. A hush of gentle breeze patted his gloomy face as he sat there under the aged flame of the forest tree with withered leaves, the only tree of its kind in the neighbourhood.

His name was Mike. Yesterday, he was a boy of nobility, gentle, courteous and happy. But was the day before. Many things had happened since. That night he was in misery, silence and agony.

The stillness of the evening air made him to sigh, for he knew that something had gone wrong. The sudden rustle of the summer wind against the thick ferns close-by made him to be aware of his consciousness. Held firmly in his right hand was a photograph of his girl. The light of the ascending full moon showed him her cute and sweet smile. As he kept on gazing her photograph he felt a sharp pain in his heart. It was so painful to bear.

"Ella, you can't do this to me. I just can't live with this kind of life anymore . . ." He whispered as his left hand touched his breast. His grip secured himself from the cool gale as well as from his misery for awhile. Even from the outside world of his.

His thought seemed to have wandered away beyond the milky ways. For a moment, he felt that his soul had been drifting in a time tunnel a decade of years back. His fantasy floated back on that Sunday morning where the whole story recalled in vision:

It was Sunday morning all right and the mass had just ended. As the space beside the main church door was packed with the outgoing congregation, he moved away to the parsonage which was only a few feet apart. There he stood, leaning against the wall and watched the people passing-by. He saw several new faces as well as old buddies of his but none was an interest to him more than what a nice girl of his.

That morning, Ella, his girl was wearing a yellow shirt with a green blouse. Her silk-looking trimmed hair touched her shoulders. There was a sweet smile on her creamy and luscious lips with her eyes so cute as if they sparked in the morning glow. What a chic complexion for a young working girl.

"Hey!"

The smiled and for some reason, he just could not take off his eyes at her sparking face. She bowed her head, shy. For a minute or two there was an awkward silence.

"Hey I just remember something," she broke the silence dulcently, "Congratulation for passing your MCE examination."

"Gee . . . , thank. You're very kind." He smiles back as he held her delicate hand and shook solemnly. "You know something . . . . ?"

"I'm afraid not. What's that?"

"It's about my result . . . you see, I couldn't make it without you . . . ."

"Mike!" She exclaimed and gave him a quick pinch on the arm. Laughter then followed: It was beautiful.

"Ella, how about a little walk back to town . . . ."

"Okayyy . . . ."

Together they left the church and walked slowly towards town. It was bright morning as the sky was cloudless. The tall palm trees that grew well along the road provided a natural shelter from the sunlight. Buzzing sound of the bees filled the shrubs where the colourful butterflies shared the morning dews. They walked so slow, letting the crowds to walk first. Soon they were far left behind the hurrying congregation.

"Mike, I feel like sitting under the tree for a while. Are you game?"

"You bet. I am."

The found several old bricks by the school fence under the shelter of a tall flame of the forest tree. There, they sat side by side facing the school buildings. It was a familiar sight and lovable place which meant a lot a young couple like them.

"Ella, do you still remember this place?"

"Of course I do. It's here where you had your bicycle tyre punctured."

On hearing her remark, he burst into laughter. Soon she too joined in. It was rather strange but true. His memory drifted back four years back on the day when he had his front bicycle tyre burst under the blazing summer sun. It was a coincidence that Ella was there, waiting for her father to fetch her home. She was then a stranger to him but as she always would, she was kind. She gave him a hand with his school books that scattered about when he fell from his bicycle. She even kept his school bag whilst he was away to have his bicycle tube changed. That was how she came to know her.

"Ella, you must have a good memory . . . , never thought you still recall that awkward noon . . . ."

She smiled as she picked up a bunch of flower that grew on her side. Looking up at his face she said." . . . but don't tell me you've forgotten those happy days we spent in school . . . ."

"No. Of course not. Instead I treasure the in my heart . . . ."

Ella lent on her shoulder and cast a long dreamy look at the school compound opposite them. Many changes had taken place but they still remember the old fence and gate, the flowers and the grasses where it used to be or grow thick long before they were shifted and trimmed short. To them it was a heavenly play ground as well as the home of their early life.

"Tell me, what you like to be life and how would you repay our school . . ."

"Me!"

Ella nodded her head gently. She looked prettier than ever as the wind blew her soft hair to the sides of her smoother and sturdy cheek. She was in her late teenage; a year younger than Mike.

"Gosh . . . . , I think I will never replace her dedication to me all those years. And never will . . . But one thing for sure; I'll go on my study in Form Sixth. Pass it with a good result and the go to university. Try to get myself a Hons. Degree before I look for job. I'm sure there's a way or another to serve her . . . 'though I just can't think of any at the moment . . ."

"Then . . ."

"Then I've settle down with you, the girl I met under the flame of the forest tree."

"Mike, you flatter me again!" Ella cried softly. Her face blushed red.

"Well, what else can I say then . . . . ? I'm a poor boy, adopted and deserted by my first girl friend . . ."

"Oh . . . Oh . . . here comes the sentimental part of my boy friend . . . ."

Ella said giving him loving smile full of understanding and care. She knew lot of his past life. So she had to be reasonable as not to hurt him again. Quickly she changed the subject of their conversation long before they walked home.

Those were some of the memories he could recall. It was a wonderful experience in life. He just could not believe why he had to bear all the pain that night.

Looking far ahead in the sky, he tried to think where he had gone wrong.

Good result, university graduate, honours degree, prospective job and happy marriage; they were all dreams. He never had a chance to achieve a good result for he failed his last HSC Examination. His GCE certificate was not an honours degree. Worst still, sitting alone under the moonlight in misery was neither a vocation nor a true life.

As for Ella, he never heard of her again since the last couple of years. He had been trying to see her but she was nowhere to be seen. Every Sunday he went to church hoping that he could meet her and explained the whole matter to her. She was not there. He met her brothers and sisters several times but they all kept silence.

Things around was not bright for him. There was silence everyway. It was yesterday when he met Ella's mother. Guess what? He had the biggest shock in life. Ella had engaged to someone. Someone she always dreams of in life. But one thing for sure that someone was not him.

At last, he managed to persuade himself to accept the reality of fate; despite of all those pressure around him. He knew, soon it would be dawn.

The cork crows filled his ears reminded him of a busy and lively life. He would be all right then. He hoped to have a fresh start when the new day comes.

25

What Life Is . . . .
(Riddle of Life)

(Composed on: 1st April 1977)

Life is but a sweet dream
Of having a friend like you
It's nothing but a big rim
Of a broken circle like U

You start with finding a friend
And end up as a love loon
With no one to talk in the rain
Like a man full of debt and loan

Day and day has gone by
Yet you never realise when
And it hurts to say goodbye
But it is all in vain

So let pause and think
What's the meaning of life?
Is it really like a link?
Between number four and five.

26

Hello Beautiful
(The Blue Invitation)

(Composed on: 5th April 1977)

Hello Beautiful
Do you mind to be my love?
For my little heart is moved
By your cute and lovely smile
And pray you'll stay for awhile

Hello Beautiful
Do you care to be my friend?
As a queen throughout my reign
I promise I'll give all you ask
My world, my life and my heart

Hello Beautiful
Do you like to be my fiancée?
And help me to reason and see
For the cure of my broken heart
To design and paint it as an art

Hello Beautiful
Do you love to be my dear wife?
To be my faithful collaborators in life
And set my empty world with love
As we give thank to the Almighty Lord.

27

So What?

(Composed on: 12th April 1977)

You are far away from my dreamy sight
Yet so close to my dear little heart
Alone in the dark, you are but a light
Shining through my heart like a dart
    So how can I say I don't need you?
    When I am in exile with the hope of you

Sometime people think me as crazy
I know that too but I never say
Let them alone and think what's fancy
Because I can reason and see
    So I think I'll keep on living alone
    Drifting with the cloud as a love loon

Yesterday has gone whilst tomorrow comes
Yet I still feel lonesome and never calm
Yet I', no more a kid but a grownup
So as my dream that never gives up
    So girl, don't you ever think and comprehend?
    If you do; onto your heart I rest my hands.

28

The Game of Death

(Composed 13th August 1977)

It had been a long time since he last set eyes on his girl. To him those halves a decade were like half his life-time in the world of patience. At last, he thought the moment for a change had come. Yet an hour before the Boeing 727 from London via Singapore touched down in the International Airport was equivalent to another hundred days to him. How he longed to have her in his arms, look at her cute face and perhaps her luscious lips.

Slowly, he slipped his cocoa-cola whilst his fingers were toying with the key of his car. His eyes focused on the most forward fan which was keeping the immediate customers fresh despite of the air conditioned canteen room on that hot summer afternoon. He sighed and sipped again. When he turned aside and came to behold the warmth expression on the faces of the hurrying passenger along the corridor on his left, it reminded him of his girl the more.

He glanced at his wrist watch and checked it with the canteen clock that hanged on his right corner. Five more minutes to go! Impatiently, he took a toss of his cool drink before he walked away. On the corridor, he passes a handful of crowd and made his way to the end of it's that overlook the runaway.

Leaning on the wall, he cast his sight through the glass window, up the flag past above the clouds. He smiled as her naughty blinking eyes appeared in fantasy. For a moment, he was all for himself, away from the noise and distraction of the modern world. He felt like in heaven somewhere beyond the blue.

The evening breeze that kept on blowing from the sea reminded him of the day four years ago before she went to Cambridge. She was then holding his hands tightly as they walked along the golden beach combing for clams and crabs. Sometime, they chased the outgoing waves and shared the joys and laughter. Throwing little shells against the in-coming waves was a part of their fun-sharing life.

As the sunset, they took a seat among the boulders that laid under the tall casuarinas trees. There they listened to the rhythm of the golden waves, the wise sermon of the casuarinas leaves and the laughter of the seagulls that nested up the cliff behind them.

He touched her soft silk-like hair and played it with his hands as she laid her head on his shoulder. Tears began to drip from her eyes before she could whisper the date of her departure across the sea. She clamped on her chest tightly as if she could do it for the next thousand years. But no one could predict how long is a thousand years for the next day she flew off with a whisper—wait for me my love.

Unexpectedly, the same whisper he echoed just before he saw a glimpse of the flying metal emerging out of the clouds. Slowly it got larger and larger, too big for a flying iron bird with rolling sound. His eyes shone with joys and his heart was flabbergasted. The wheel popped out gently under its wing and screeched a bit. A minute later, the plane taxied alongside the corridor on which he was on.

"Oh God, how am I going to thank you for these . . ." He whispered as he saw her stepping out of the plane's door. He did shade a few tears. Ignoring the noise, he waves his hands but she did not waved back. Reluctantly, he withdrew his hand and gazed her as she walked towards the Immigration Office. "May . . . maybe she is not Teresa!"

His sight darted among the passenger but no one was familiar except that young lady with a cute face. Although her hairs had turned light blonde but it was still hers. He was truly sure of it.

The next moment, he found himself standing outside the Immigration Office. He peeped among the passengers in vain before he walked over to the next door but still he could not find her. But all of a sudden, he ran onto someone unexpectedly. Quickly he turned apologized politely; "Oh my God! I'm sorry. I do not . . . Teresa!"

Teresa still clutching her right arm gave a faint smile and stared at him; "Teresa . . . me?"

"Of course, you're Theresa, are you?"

"Yeah! That's me . . . have I seen you somewhere before?"

"Why, don't you recognize me . . . ? I'm Steve." He said with a smile in his lips and birdsong in his heart.

"Steve . . ." She whispered as she step aside closed to a young man. "Steve . . . of course, I know you: you're our former Head boy when I was still in a secondary school"

Steve wanted to go on saying something but he hesitated. He smelt something had gone wrong.

"Yeas, how nice!" she breathed off at last, "Alan, my former Head Boy; Steve. And this is my husband, Alan."

They shook hand. Alan smiled. But Steve did not consider it as a smile, it was a grim. He knew it. "That's right. We got married a week ago!"

"Oh . . . . Con . . . Congratulation!" he snapped. His face had turned pale as if he saw a ghost. He just could not believe it yet someone used to say: seeing is believing!

Alan and Teresa would not bother of this wise saying for them they had a programmed of their own. Making an excuse was not at all rare especially when it came on to personal matter. They apologized and left, holding hands as they walked towards the taxi parking space leaving Steve alone in perplexity.

"But . . . but how about the letter,. It says she is going home to marry me. And now she is . . . ." Darts of reasons poked his confused brain to its worse. Sweet flowed from his forehead with warm and humiliation. "No, it's not going to end here; I got to make sure that she is not the real Teresa."

Bursting out of the International Airport, he jumped into the front seat of his new sport cat that parked outside. He ignited its spark and drove like mad. In fact, he was. He was driving his car in a grand prix with a prize of life and death. Yet, preferred death for there was no sunshine without Teresa. A hundred meters away, the traffic light pricked to show its red colour in vain. His car shrieked and hit its victim. He felt a hush of gentle and warm breeze before he could hear the fading sound of the church bell. No one could help him for he had made his last score.

Early next morning, the doctor's door suddenly burst opened with Teresa came running in followed by her family. She was still clinging on to the doctor chest with tears on her eyes. When her mother took her from his arms, her sisters crowded in to comfort her. Holding her mother, she refused to be consoled. From her faint voice, the doctor came to know what she asked for.

"What's going on!" asked the doctor to her father after they had gone to another adjusting room. "What's your daughter got to do with Steve?"

"I just don't know how to begin, doctor. I just don't know."

"Please, Mister Frank," said the doctor trying to calm his client's impatient. "Here, come have a drink before you tell me what's happens . . ."

Mister Frank, Teresa's father shocked his head as he wiped off the sweets that streamed down his bold head. He sipped the cold water before he explained the reason why.

"Doc, you won't believe this but it's true. Steve is my son-in-law; Theresa's fiancé. He is supposed to marry her this weekend . . . but why? Why must . . . ."

"Please Mister Frank. Don't be carried away. Take it easy, you might make the circumstances worst." Advised the doctor again fearing he might jeopardize her daughter. Mister Frank walked towards the window. He could not bear to hear the wail of her daughter from the other room, no more.

"But why Teresa and Alan must do that foolish game." He went on, "You see doc. I sent Steve to welcome Teresa at the airport yesterday evening. When she arrived accompanied by her cousin, Alan, they behave in an unreasonable manner . . . they ignored him and pretended to be a newly-we couple which broke his heart. You see, they don't mean to do it seriously, she just wanted to tease him . . ."

"And kill a soul" Another familiar voice interrupted Mister Frank remark.

"Steve? Steve . . . ! Thanks God. You're alright!" exclaimed Mister Frank as he behold a young man, looked familiar and walked like Steve. At the sometime, the door opened and Teresa came in. Still crying she threw herself at the young man's feet. Her gripped tighten holding her feet and refuse to let if off.

"Steve . . . . Steve . . . . I, I'm sorry. We're just joking. I've not married yet. I . . . . I come home to marry you"

All stood in silence despite of a few sobbing moment.

"Steve . . . Steve, why don't you answer me. Don't you forgive me, Steve please, say something."

The young man bent down and holding her hands, he pulled her up gently. He embarrassed her and burst into tears.

Everyone did share the moment of sobbing.

Slowly, the Youngman let off her hand, still in tears he whispered loud enough to be heard by the inhabitants of the room, "Sister, you're beautiful and sincere at heart but you have made a grave mistake. You're playing with a game of death!"

The young man turned aside and banged the wall with tears in his eyes before he entered the room from which he had come out of.

Teresa sank to her feet, a moment before her mother could catch her from falling. Teresa's sisters came to the rescue. Theresa's dad tried to pursuit him but the doctor prevented him.

"Why . . . why are you stopping me to see my son-in-law doc? Why?" exclaimed Mister Frank in rage. "Do you want to kill my daughter . . . ."

"No, I don't mean that,' begged the doctor calmly, "I got a reason why!"

"Reason, I don't care for your reason. I too have a reason to see Steve . . . He is my son-in-law. Don't you hear me?"

The doctor was still insisting not to open the door when a voice called in from inside, "Doctor, don't trouble yourself. You've done your best. Let them open the door if that's what they want . . . ."

"Steve . . . can't you forgive Teresa?"

"Sir. If I'm Steve I would have hail to your request before you ask but I'm not." said the young man who stood beside the long operation room.

"What have gone into you, Steve? Are you mad? Are you saying you're not Steve? Who are you then, a ghost?"

"I'm not a ghost sir!" introduced the young man, "Nor Steve. I'm Steven, Steve twin brother!"

For a moment, everyone in the room except doctor became puzzled. All were still even Teresa.

"But . . . but where's Steve?"

Without uttering a word, Steven bite his dry lips as he controlled his tears. Slowly he turned behind and uncovered the face of his dead brother who was still lying on the operation table.

On seeing Steve's pale face, Teresa gave a shriek as he pushed his sisters aside and rushed onto the operation table. She embraced her finance corpse. She cried still clinging to her body refused to be comforted. Her voice hoarse until it was no more than a whisper.

Her feet, hand and lips turned cold and pale. Her heart beat refused to beat no more. Before her parents could recover from their own shock, Teresa breathed her last.

Realizing from the too late moment which cost them a dear life of another soul, a girl, they could do nothing but cry. At least such feeling expressed the whole game of death.

29

A Couple More Years

(Composed on the 23rd August 1977)

Nobody seem to understand me,
not even you, Honey, so
I guess I've got a couple more years
And that's all . . .
For I have no chances to fly,
I have come from a windy road
Much further than what you've
A refugee in the land of mine
No places to fall . . .
You said you have been to somewhere
I was there too and found that . . . .
Nobody was there at all . . . . So
I guess I've got a couple more years
And that's all . . . .

30

Blue Interlude

(Composed on the 9th October 1977)

"Oh . . . No!" I just can not concentrate with my work!"

He sighed and stretched his arms high and wide. He could hear his joints cracked like a dry stick. And before he put on his concave photo grey spectacles, he rubbed his eyes with his fingers. But still his eyes were getting misty; he seemed to be reading a double letter. Taking off his glasses again, he blinked his eyes several time before he put on.

"Oh, damn it! It just doesn't work!" he cursed. Throwing his pen into a black James-Bond that lay opened on the rattan chair, he took the last toss of his cold lemon drink. As his mind was not at all peaceful and seemed reading the same sentence for the fourth time, he became very frustrated.

Tightened his jaw, he glanced around his desk and room. His room was small and messy. Although he was afresh member of the National Press Family, he felt proud of it. Now he realised that it was killing him slowly.

"My God, it doesn't work either!" This time, he packed all his papers inside his bag. A few minutes later, most of his two hours work ended in the paper basket. Tucking his bag under his bed, he snatched his mini cassette-recorder from the drawer before he stormed out of room grumbling. He decided to quit as a reporter awhile.

From his press-quarter tucked at the end of the busy town, he determined to stroll away from the distraction of the modern civilisation. His ears were filled with murmurs of people clattering and the sound of the machine type-writers. Thus he did not care where he was going as long as away from the torturing life of his. He wanted to hear and see something new, pleasant and romantic for a poor soul.

Without realising, he reached the hilltop that overlooked the plain. Down there was a small valley where a couple of press-quarter were situated. As he was facing west so the right building, second floor, room number seven was his apartment. Through the transparent glass window, he still could see his books and clips of newsletters, faintly.

But he cared little of it now for his heart was beginning to get acquaintance with nature.

It was really a blessed evening. The cool breeze was blowing onshore and felt like cream on his face. The sweet fragrant flowers with purple-red colour from the neighbouring bushes filled his sense. Half a mile ahead stretched the golden-blue South China Sea with silver sparking horizon. The reflection of the setting sunlight on the roofs of the terrace rest house that occupied the southern end of the beach reminded him of the Milky Way above.

He lay down on the green lawn. Closing his eyes he emptied his troubles mind in an exchange of the natural gifts: The romantic songs of the yellow bird; the solemn whisper of the wind and the gentle warmth of the sunset. So absorbed with the free gift of God that he failed to find out where he was: right within the fenceless lawn of a bungalow.

"Puppy, puppy, where are you?" A gentle and sweet voice echoed behind the bushes. "Puppy . . . come here, Puppy?"

Still he ignored it. It was getting louder and louder before it ceased. And when he opened his eye-lids, to his surprised; a small white-fur Japanese puppy was gazing at him. So near that he could hear it's breathe as it waged its short tail.

At the same moment, a cute, lovely face emerged from the scrub. It was a girl dressed in an Arabian blue evening gown. He felt flabbergasted. "I'm sorry", she snapped shyly, "I'm looking for puppy . . ."

"Oh!" He exclaimed softly not knowing what else to utter. And whilst he was getting ready to rise up, the naught creatures hopped onto his lap and licked his face. He felt so embarrassed that he blushed.

"I see, seems that puppy has found a new master now . . ."

"Gosh, I think you're right!" He said trying to cool his nerve from the moment of an unexceptional. Gently, he strokes its head with his palm before he handed it back onto her smoother arms.

"Say, she's a beauty! I wish I have one!"

She smiled sweetly. "He is not she; he is he!"

"Opps . . . . , I'm sorry!"

Her hair was short and it danced in the breeze like a black silk. There was something in her eyes that he could not understand." By the way, you must be the new guy working in the National Press Family".

"Err, yea!" He hesitated, "but, how do you know . . . ?"

"Well, just say I saw you working out of the of the Press quarter half an hour ago."

"Wow! What do you know! Somebody is sticking somebody's eyes on me now a day!" She smiled, "By the way, I'm . . . ."

". . . Jerry?" She snapped before he could complete his sentence.

He became more surprised. "Well, don't tell me you've met me before because I haven't!"

"But my daddy has! He is the Managing Director of the National Press Family", she added, "You know, he used to tell mum once awhile about you; a hard-working and tactful guy . . . !"

He stood there in perplexity, trying not to believe that he was face to face with his boss' daughter. He then drew his sight from her toes to her head unbelievable. Her evening gown fluttered in the air as a fairy princess. Yet she was there as if she was an old friend of his.

"Well, you don't mean to tell your dad that I still haven't finished my report assignments, do you? Miss . . . ."

". . . . Tracy!" She said lovingly. There was something in her voice that caught his attention of not letting it to slip away. She too had a reason of her own. Or probably they knew they had something in common.

Together, they sat down and shared the romantic evening. Not all could understand why such unexpected meeting ended so merrily. Yet the moment of interlude had changed his perishing life into a world of utopia and melody.

As the time ticked-by, the sun set for a short rest. It has witnessed and pacified another episode of human life of which it deserved a good night slumber. Before the first star twinkled, he kissed her hands as he bid her goodnight.

Both had found what they had been looking for in the life of the youth. Yet that was only a part of it since they still had another day to keep . . . .

31

The Last Wail

(Composed on 25th October 1977)

I keep on telling myself . . .
    I have nothing else to care
No more smile and grief . . . .
    For they've passed and gone
Even the flowers refuse . . . .
    To bloom and bear fruit
I have seen many tears flows
    As clear as the stream of spring
So many cloudy days . . .
    No breeze, no more bird song
Only merciless gale breaking
    The branch of hope as it passes by
Fallen to the lonely ground
    Trodden and crushed by memories
Yet I can not look back in regret
    For I've done my part to the last wail . . . .

32

(Composed on 26th October 1977)

How I love and care for you
What a memory to behold . . .
. . . . all those unforgettable moment
When we first met and learnt ABC
. . . yet it was only a dream
Soon it has vanished in the cool mist
Like a mirage in the waterless desert
So real to look at, so persuasive
Yet all are emptied, meaningless
. . . for the scar is still visible
A token to ponder in the sea
Of life . . . I've learn to live
Never to be deceived again

33

The Freedom of Seagull

(Composed on the 27th October 1977)

How I wish to be a seagull,
    So white the feathers so pure,
In heart like a new born babe,
    No worry, no spot and guile,
I can spread myself in the gentle
    Warmth of kindness and joys,
And discover the blue . . . high up,
    In the sky of life bounty,
How I love to glide around . . .
    The green atoll in search of friendship,
And race with the nimble sea current
    . . . . in search of truth and bread,
For that is what I'm for . . .
    I like the strong surf breaker,
Which scatters the stubborn waves?
    And indicate them all for tomorrow,
In the book of patience and endurance,
    Lest to forget the Lord God,
To whom I owe myself and deeds.

34

For You Sweet Heart

(Composed on the 27th October 1977)

Beautiful is the time we once shared
    How I look at you and called your name
I can not forget those happy school times
    And linger the memories of long, long time
I've seen your eyes that cute little stars
    Which guide me through my early life?
Although you may not understand but
    God knows how I adore you, honey
Now that you've gone, you're still with me
    It may not be the same, only recollections
How I wish you'll come home to me
    I long to see you and feel your warm shake
I don't want to miss you for so long
    Probably I may be late but I don't care
I've love you and always be
    I know I can always have you in . . . .
Memories of those years we had before
    Should I miss you here on earth?
I shall wait for you in heaven at the gate . . .
    Till you come, take good care.

35

Hidden Passion

(Composed on the 16th November 1977)

From the corner of your eyes
    I can see the future of mine
So elegant and lovely to behold,
    Like the sunshine of summer;
Though your smile is not yet for me,
    Yours alone and no more
But I keep on reaching you,
    Through patient and prayer;
Maybe you don't comprehend,
    For there is silence everywhere;
Yet my love for you will,
    Cherish and fade no more;
With my faith, hope and love,
    It will be like treasure;
Keep where no moth will endow.

36

To My Love

(Composed on the 17th November 1977)

Love . . . .
Could you but spare me a moment?
Help me to discard these memories of mine
For wherever I go I think of you,
No matter in the air, sea or land.

Love . . . .
I'm tired of caring
I want to be free like the seagull
Where no more guile, worry and sin,
Only the feeling of a freeborn man
Living in the land of the sunshine vale . . .

Love . . . .
I have been toiling for years
Doing odd thing to let thing slip by
All but you are gone in my memories
I care not yet it hurts more
Now I can not but endure . . . .

37

Born Loser

(Composed 22nd November 1977)

Rush of wind swept across his path as he made his way to the open gate. Not even a dog was in sight. And except for the buzzing sound of the yellow scrubs that lined along the school pavement, everything was quiet, at least for the time being.

"Gosh, I hope I can make my way to the bus stop before it rain," he thought as he hastened his step. Soon he could feel the rain whistling as if approached within the dark creeping clouds. Raising his left arm to shield his proto-glass spectacle from being blown by the gale as well as to protect his face from the flying leaves and dust, he quickened his pace.

But he was not lucky. Before he could pass the gate, the rain had already started dripping like melted snow. He did not even have an umbrella. Across the road laid the dry place of refuge, the bus stop. Yet, as he put on his step on the slippery road for a dash, a sharp horn honked somewhere on his right, a warning.

"God, I sure get wet in this rain," he prowled as he withdrew back to the sidewalk reluctantly. Then string of vehicles blocked his gateway from the threatening cloud. The cloud extended its arm of darts of water drops before it huddled on him mercilessly. He felt the liquid-string penetrated his skin as it soaked onto his all white school uniform. It was so cool to bear.

Thinking that his star had deserted him, he turned aside for cover on the school garage close by. He hesitated. All at a sudden, he found the rain drop had ceased to batter his back.

"Here, let us share my umbrella," echoed he turned, there beside him stood a young school girl holding as Arabian-blue umbrella.

From her fair face came a sweet smile. Her eyes were cute looking and sparkling like an emerald. She looked familiar.

Caught by the unexpected moment, he was flabbergasted. There was something in her eyes that made him flushed. "Oh, thank you . . ." He whispered, so soft that he doubted if he had heard it himself.

She nodded her head in smile as she stepped closer to him and felt the warm of her tender skin when it touched his. Every word that he was going to utter stuck in his throat, as the car continued to honk their horn: a tribute to the new couple being stranded in the middle of nowhere.

At last, the crossed the road safely. "Say, are we lucky! Here is the bus!" she said, folding her umbrella. He stood there smiling without saying a word. He was shy.

The next moment, it stopped and they hopped into the bus. Crowded as it was, they stood side by side. And when they had their bus tickets inspected, they rode in silence. But deep in his heart, a glow of blue flourished within his lonesome heart.

In the following days, he had not seen her again. Sometime, he waited late in the afternoon. Hoping she would pass that way again from her school nearby yet she never turned up. Not for the being. Still the seed of hidden love at first sight had already bore its flower of endurance.

Late one afternoon, the moment of expectation came to a reality. Unfortunately, the bus he was on packed with passengers and he had to stand away from her. Beside she was sitting with a friend of hers. And friend was a boy. Sadness prevailed deep in his heart as he missed the chance he longed to have. Little by little the feeling of uneasiness crept into his heart.

Soon he was adrift inside his imaginations in the treasons world of outcast. Two years ago, he lost his girl to someone and had not seen her ever since. It had really taken a great deal of his trust. Yet his love was greater than a pearl. He had been bearing the burden soft and low no matter how it hurt him. The moment he found his new find, had brightened his misery. Now it happened again.

It was months later when he came to meet her again for the third time. The moment was then too late. He was riding in a bus too with her new find, her finance. From the rear seat, he could see her handsome champion enjoying the morning trip.

The fresh morning breeze kept on blowing her short trimmed hair against her soft cheek. The sturdy shoulder of hers lent over gently on her fiancé's broad shoulder. Whispers kept on streaming from her lips embroidered with blinking naughty eyes and sweet smile. Yet to him, her smile was then no longer a blessing but a mockery like mockery horn of the cars that they heard at their first meeting. The coolness of the steel wall of the bus on which he lent and the chilling breeze of the misty morning reminded him of the coolness of the monsoon shower before she turned up with her umbrella on that rainy afternoon.

Unbearable to keep his sight on the girl he once trusted, he turned aside. Out there in the field was displayed a fantasy of the past in a twinkle of an insight. It was so sad to feel yet so beautiful to behold.

"So long Karen. It's nice to know you . . . ." He whispered. So soft that he doubt whether he had heard it himself; just like the time when he uttered his appreciation to the girl who offered him a share in the temporary shelter within the Arabian blue umbrella in the first place.

38

The Tale of Christmas
SPECIAL

(Composed on the 11th December 1977)

It was afternoon, a few minutes after lunch hour. At first, the office in which he worked was quiet. He was alone; all his workmates had not yet arrived from their afternoon refreshment. Not even a whisper was heard. Faintly, the stillness was disturbed by echoes of a distant pace. It was getting louder and louder. There was something familiar with the sound; firm taps of a high-heel sandal.

"Gosh!" he breathed hard as if something was keeping him from the free grasp of air. He then tightened his grip at the edge of his office desk and forced himself to concentrate his afternoon nap. He could not.

He was experiencing a strange feeling vibrating within his nerve, a feeling that he hate to have especially at a lonesome moment as this. Hesitating, he raised his head and glanced towards the doorway.

There, she walked in with a plastic bag clamped tightly between her smooth arms. Her short-trimmed hair hung loosely and brushed her fair shoulders as she walked. Her eyes were so cute to look at. From her luscious lips was a sweet smile no matter how hard she tried to hide. Refusing to acknowledge the pain of his bitten lip, he turned aside, bowed and buried his head between his folded arms. It was too much for him.

The girl was Rita, his new workmate. He had been trying hard to ignore her presence ever since he first came to work there, a couple of months ago. Unlike the rest of his pretty office-mates, she was familiar. He knew he had not seen her before but still it did not make any difference; she reminded him of someone dear in heart. That little pretty face, those lovely gestures whenever she moved around, her sweet gentle voice and honey-like smile that she possessed were a resemblance to his old nearly forgotten girl. It all happened a year ago before he graduated from the High School.

It was the most memorable time that he ever had in his life. Eurphasia, his old girlfriend was very much like Rita. Together with Eurphasia, they spend many good times, not to mention the season of Happy Tiding.

He still remembered how they celebrated the Christmas; sharing the joys and blessing, singing the Christmas carols and a beautiful shopping afternoon.

"No, no, you must not open your eyes before I told you so", Eurphasia insisted him.

"Okay, you bet!" he snapped closing his eyelids. He knew she had a surprise for him. He waited. He could felt the smoothness of her hand touching his and slowly she folded his palm after placing a hard metal in . . .

"Now, you can open your eyes, slowly now . . ." she said accompanied by a friendly laughter. He opened his eyes. Unbelievable, he saw a golden chair with heart-shape pendent engraved with cross and beautiful designs. Inside the necklace pendent was their colour photograph. "It's for you, Honey; Merry Christmas . . . !"

He gave a short exclamation. Then he placed his arms around her and she hugged him willingly. "Merry Christmas to you too, dear", he murmured as he kissed her cherry-like lips.

He was still gripping the necklace his girlfriend's Christmas special gift when he heard his boss called him. Discarding those memories of yesterday, he rose up and made his way to the adjacent room. He could not recalled how longed he was in there. But when he came out of the room it was nearly four in the afternoon.

The first thing that he noticed when he returned to the mess office room was a strange sight. All the other desks were partly emptied. Most of the clerks had flocked to the front desk. "Hey . . . Joe! Want to some Christmas card".

"Who has for sale?"

"Rita has. You better come over or you'll have to get for yourself in town."

Reluctantly, he walked over to the next couple of desk row. He peeped. There, in the middle he saw Rita was busy distributing carton after carton of Christmas cards to her friends as a discount rate. He stood aside as he left the rest of his colleagues did the buying.

"Hey, want to have a Christmas special?" Rita snapped shyly. That was the first time she talked to him ever since he joined the firm.

"Emmm . . . may be. Can I have a look first?"

"Sure, why not!" He walked closer and had the carton handed to him. One after another, he sorted those cards in the box. It was a strange occasion for silence did bridge their thought. From the corner of his eyes, he could examine her sparkling face which had kept him isolated for the last even weeks.

"If you can't make up your mind, I think I can help you to decide on one!" she said politely when she realised that it was beyond his judgement. "And I recommend you to have this. You know, it's beautifully printed and coloured".

Surprisingly, when he looked at it; it was what he had been looking for: A real Christmas card with beautiful designs, poetry greeting and green colour on the back ground.

"Say, how much it cost?" He snapped looking up directly at her face for the first time. Their eyes met and she bowed her head, shy. He handed her the payment gently in her palm.

"Thank you. You're very kind". He swore he saw her bite her lips and could hardly smile. The he moved towards his own desk where he unfolded the specially chosen Christmas card and read its wording solemnly:

JOY BE YOURS AT
    CHRISTMAS
AND LOVE THAT
    FILLS THE HEART
WITH ALL THE
    HEAVENLY BLESSING
THAT NEVER
    SHALL DEPART

But when he turned towards the doorway, there he saw Rita was leaving the office with a handsome guy from the adjacent section.

About the Author

ABOKSAN is a pseudonym of noel MICHAEL LISIUS abok. Writing poems and short stories are one of his old diehard hobbies since school days. Others hobbies includes travelling and photography.

ABOKSAN has ventured into Novel writing recently rekindling his childhood passion for advance writing which he rediscovered upon retirement lately.

Since retirement, **ABOKSAN** is residing in Keningau, Sabah, Malaysia with his wife, Emily Francis Asing and host of siblings.

Currently, **ABOKSAN** is editing some of his literary works which he kept in the closet for so long. Some of it dated during the seventies which he hopes to have them published in due time for the benefits of the young and not so young.

ABOKSAN dreams that some day, one of his novels will be a master piece and probably be a box office movie . . .

ABOKSAN—I MISS YOU—is a collection of poems and short stories which was written within a span of five or so. **(1975-1979).**

TO BE SUCCESSFUL, TURNS YOUR NIGHTMARE INTO SWEET DREAMS.

.Quotation: ABOKSAN